NO MATTER HOW YOU PLAY IT

story by Lisa Olsson

photographs by Tracy Wheeler

collages by Mary Lynn Carson

HARCOURT BRACE & COMPANY

Orlando   Atlanta   Austin   Boston   San Francisco   Chicago   Dallas   New York
Toronto   London

TRUMPET

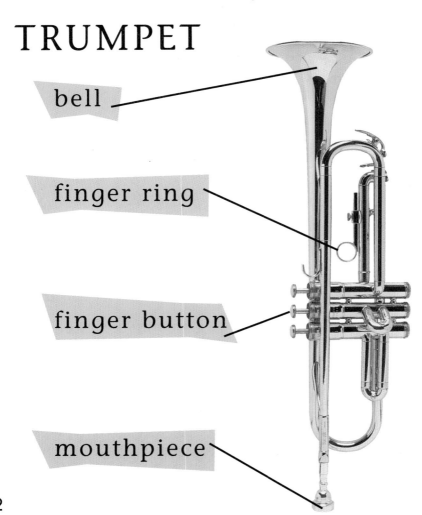

bell

finger ring

finger button

mouthpiece

Trumpet

The trumpet is a brass instrument.
It has only three finger buttons,
but it can play many loud sounds.

VIOLIN

string

neck

sound hole

bow

Violin

The violin is the smallest stringed instrument. Moving the bow across the strings can make soft sounds.

5

GUITAR

string

neck

sound hole

The guitar is another stringed
instrument.
It has six strings that are
plucked or strummed.

DRUM

drumhead

shell

sticks

A drum can be played
with sticks or hands.
The drumbeat keeps the
rhythm of the music.

PIANO

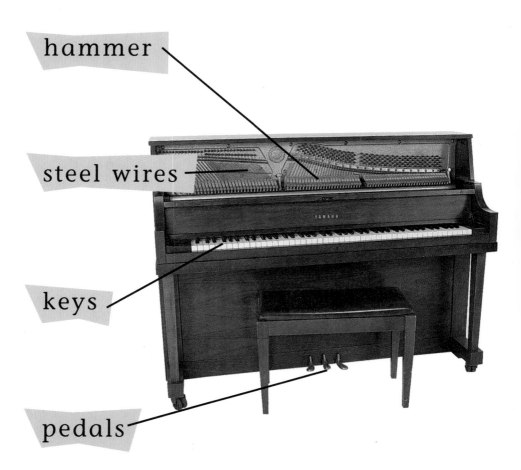

hammer

steel wires

keys

pedals

The piano makes many high and low sounds.
When the keys are pressed, small hammers hit the steel wires.

11

You can play music softly, loudly, slowly, or quickly. There are many ways to make music.